INSPIRING STEM CAREERS

FOR KIDS 8-12 YEARS OLD
ENGLISH EDITION

THIS BOOK BELONGS TO:

_____

_____

_____

_____

INSPIRING STEM CAREERS

FOR KIDS 8-12 YEARS OLD
ENGLISH EDITION

BY
ELIZABETH SHELBY

Kindly visit the author's website,
www.letscolorimaginations.com
to see more of her work and even get a free
22-page activity book if you join the mailing list.

"What are you good at doing? There is a career for you depending on your skills. Here are 30 careers that you may have in the future."

Web Designer

Creates designs and layouts for websites.
They make it easy for people to get around a website,
whether they want to buy products or to learn about a topic.

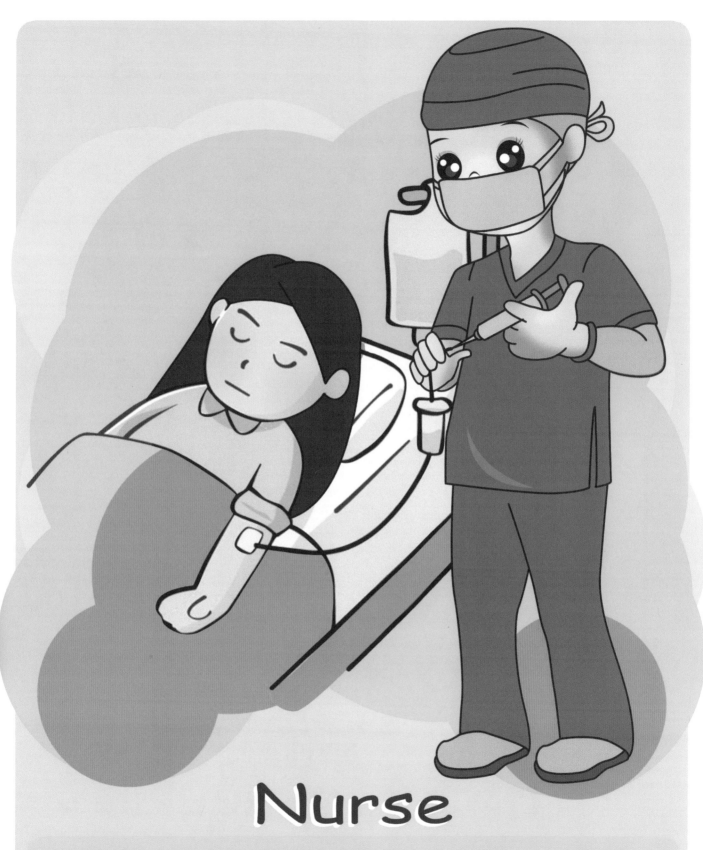

Nurse

A nurse is a person who is trained to care for sick and injured people. They work with doctors and other health care workers to make patients get better as well as keep patients fit and healthy.

Entrepreneur

Someone who chooses to create and run a business.
They try to create things that solve problems.
When people buy a product the business makes money.

Teacher

A teacher teaches children in a classroom at a school.
They help children learn mathematics, language, science,
social studies, etc.

Firefighter

Trained to control and put out fires. They work quickly as a team to keep fires from spreading. They control fire by connecting hoses to fire hydrants and operating pumps to power the hoses. They may also need to rescue people who are trapped inside burning buildings.

Robotics Engineer

A robotics engineer thinks of ways that people can use robots.
They then design, build, or repair robots.

Veterinarian

A doctor for animals.
They prevent, diagnose, and treat animal diseases.
They can perform surgery and advise drugs for animals.
They can keep your favorite pet happy and healthy.

Biotechnology Scientist

A biotechnology scientist looks closely at plants and animals.
Their main job is to take what they find to help sick people.
They work together to make cures and treatments. They save lives
and help improve people's health.

Police Woman

A police officer's job is to enforce laws, solve crimes, and protect property. They also help with emergencies such as when people are injured in a car accident.

Software Developer

A software developer is a person who creates software.
Software tells computers what to do or how to perform a task.
It helps make your phone, tablet, and personal computer easier
for you to use.

Plumber

A plumber is a person whose job is to connect and repair things such as water and drainage pipes, baths, and toilets.

Physical Therapist

A physical therapist helps injured people. They work to decrease pain, improve movement, and help people return to daily life after an injury. They teach people exercises that can help them regain strength and show people how to prevent future injuries.

Musician

A musician plays, sings, or composes songs.
They often play an instrument such as the guitar,
keyboard, drums, etc.

Electrician

An electrician works on electrical power.
They install, test, and maintain wiring, lighting systems, and fixtures
in homes and businesses.

Nanotechnology Scientist

A nanotechnology scientist studies very tiny things called atoms and subatomic particles. Atoms make up everything that occupies space in the universe called matter. They study those things to make new materials, equipment, or drugs.

Chef

A chef is a person who cooks professionally in a restaurant.
They are in charge of everyone who works in the kitchen.
They are responsible for everything about the food to be served.

Mathematician

A mathematician works in the field of mathematics. They study numbers, data, and theories to solve practical problems in business, government, engineering, and science.

Actor

An actor is a person who acts a part in a play, a movie,
or a radio or television program.

Parent

A parent's job is to care for, discipline, teach, raise, guide, and nurture their children. They teach kids about basic manners and how to treat others. They help children to be good persons.

Scientist

A scientist tries to understand how our world or other things work. They make observations, ask questions, and do extensive research work to find the answers to many questions.

Astronaut

An astronaut is a person who travels out to outer space through a spacecraft to conduct experiments and gather information.

Genetic Engineer

A genetic engineer studies genes and how things grow and change. Genes allow our bodies to have different traits such as the color of your eyes. A genetic engineer would make genetic changes to create solutions for problems like fighting diseases such as cancer or diabetes.

Artificial Intelligence Engineer

An artificial intelligence engineer creates machines and software that can think for themselves. They help computers to learn and solve problems.

Dentist

A dentist spots problems with people's teeth, gums, and mouth.
They also clean teeth and correct bite issues.

Aerospace Engineer

Designs, builds, tests, maintains, and enhances aircrafts, spacecrafts, satellites, missiles, and other weapon systems. One type of aerospace engineer is the aeronautical engineer who specializes in flight in the Earth's atmosphere. Another type is the astronautical engineer who specializes in flight outside of the Earth's atmosphere.

Environmental Engineer

Improves environmental and human health by properly
managing and reducing waste as well as developing
better ways to recycle. They also study pollution problems
in the air, water, and soil and create solutions
to reduce or eliminate pollution.

Information Security Analyst

Protects a company's top secret information stored electronically from hackers. They install protective software and perform security measures on the company's computer systems.

Climatologist

Conducts long-term studies on weather patterns to learn about the Earth's climate and foretell future climate changes. From their findings, they would guide society in correspondingly planning activities, growing crops, constructing buildings and infrastructures that can endure adverse weather.

Actuary

Figures out the costs of risk, meaning bad things that can happen like disability, death, loss in investment, etc. They work for companies that require financial risk management such as insurance companies, hospitals, banks.

Augmented Reality Engineer

Produces various elements in the computer such as 3D graphics, videos, audio, and text to create a life-like world that people can experience through a device such as an AR headset. Their work is often used for video games, entertainment, advertising, education, architecture.

If you'd like to learn more about careers, you may discuss careers with a more knowledgeable grown-up. Or if you're lucky, you might even find someone who does a job you like, and you can talk to them about their job.

Please visit www.letscolorimaginations.com
If you join our mailing list
download a free 22 page activity book.

Check out my other books at www.letscolorimaginations.com

Magical World of Princess Coloring Book
(For Girls ages 4-8 years)

Magical World of Princess Coloring Book
(For Girls ages 8-12 years)

Princess, Unicorn, Mermaid, Fairy and Pegasus
Activity Book (For Kids ages 4-8) Volume 1, 2, 3

Princess, Unicorn, Mermaid, Fairy and Pegasus
Activity Book (For Kids ages 8-12) Volume 1, 2, 3

I Can Be Anything I Want To Be
Inspiring Careers for Girls
(Coloring Book)

Can Be Anything I Want To Be
Inspiring Careers for Boys
(Coloring Book)

Check out my other books at www.letscolorimaginations.com

Unicorn Coloring Book (For Kids ages 4-8)

Unicorn Coloring Book (For Kids ages 8-12)

Mermaids Coloring Book (For Kids ages 4-8)

Mermaids Coloring Book (For Kids ages 8-12)

Magical World of Fairies Coloring Book
(For Kids ages 4-8)

Magical World of Fairies Coloring Book
(For Kids ages 8-12)

Enchanted Fairy World Coloring Book
(For Kids ages 8-12 & Adults)

Illustrated books

Grown up me ,will be
Inspiring careers for kids 4-8y/o

When I grow up I want to be.
Inspiring stem careers for kid 8-11y/o
Coloring books

Chibi girls coloring book

Check out my other books at
www.letscolorimaginations.com

Zendoddle Designs
for kids 8-12
Careers Coloring Book

I hope you enjoyed this book.
Please let me know by leaving a review.

Printed in Great Britain
by Amazon

24692503R10025